The Legend of Dave the Villager 23

By Dave Villager

Seventh Edition (February 2023)

www.davethevillager.com
www.facebook.com/davevillager

Email me at: davevillagerauthor@gmail.com

The Legend of Dave the Villager is published by Pawkins Publishing.

BOOK TWENTY-THREE:
Attack of the Phantoms

PROLOGUE

"What are we going to do with the boat?" Carl asked.

Dave looked back at the white yacht, which was bobbing up and down in the water.

"Well, I guess we'll need to go back at some point," said Dave. "Let's hide it somewhere, and hope we remember where it is."

The yacht had brought them to a beach made from hills of stone blocks and gravel. There was no sand, it was raining heavily and the waves were crashing against the stone. Dave, Carl and Spidroth had brought the yacht as close to the stone shore as possible before jumping off, but even so they had landed in the water and got soaked before climbing up onto the stony beach.

"You two make us some shelter," Dave yelled, trying to make his voice heard in the fierce rain. "I'll take care of the yacht."

Dave took a diamond pickaxe out from his bag and dug out a small cave in one of the stone hills, low enough so that the water from the ocean flowed into it. Then he swam over to the boat, climbed up and went into the cabin.

"Er, computer, go into that little cave over there," said Dave, talking to the computer screen.

"Ok," said the computer. Then the yacht slowly crept forward, going into the little cave that Dave had made.

"Are you going to be alright here?" Dave asked the computer.

"Yes," said the computer.

"Er, well I'll leave the cave open in case you want to sail off anywhere," said Dave.

"I won't," said the computer. "I am a simple computer with no needs of my own. But thank you."

Dave went above deck. The cave was only small and would only be visible from the ocean, so the yacht should be safe. He jumped down into the water and swam through the cave, back onto the beach.

How am I going to remember where on the beach the cave is if I ever come back? Dave wondered. And then he had an idea. He took blocks of netherrack from his bag and placed them above the entrance to the cave.

Further up the stony beach, Dave could see that Spidroth and Carl had already built a small wooden hut, and there was warm light coming from inside. He ran over, eager to get out of the rain. When he got inside, Carl and Spidroth had already started a fire with a block of netherrack and built three beds.

Dave joined his friends on the floor, all of them huddling around the fire.

"Well, we've now gone further than anyone has ever been," said Dave. "All the maps say there is no land this far west, and we've found some. How exciting is that!"

"I'd be more excited if it wasn't so wet," said Carl. "Maybe that's why this place was never recorded on any maps: all the explorers who got here just decided to give up and go home."

"It is interesting," said Spidroth. "Even in my time it was believed that there was nothing this far west. We are exploring uncharted lands."

"The only uncharted land I'm interested in exploring is my bed," said Carl, wriggling out of his diamond golem armor and then getting under his bed covers. Dave put out the fire with his boot, and then he and Spidroth got into their beds as well.

Dave always felt extra snug when he was tucked up in bed when the weather was bad outside. He could see the rain splattering against the windows and hear the wind whistling, but he was lovely and warm and comfy.

Before long, he'd drifted off to sleep, and began to dream.

Dave dreamed he was back in his hometown, the way it had been before Steve had destroyed it. He was sitting in his garden, laughing and joking with all his friends. Carl and Spidroth were there, but so was Porkins, Alex, Robo-Steve, Captain Nitwit and Little Billy.

"Anyone for some apple juice?"

It was his dad, holding a tray of glasses. His mum was there too, both of them smiling.

"We used to enjoy things too," said a gloomy voice. "Before we were cursed."

Dave turned around and saw a small crowd of endermen.

"Us too," said a deep, derpy voice.

Dave turned and saw a group of zombies.

"Don't forget ussss," hissed another voice.

Dave turned and saw a group of skeletons.

Dave was no longer in his garden now, and all his friends were gone. He was in the endless, bleak yellow desert of The End, with a black sky above him. Endermen were everywhere.

Dave looked up and saw purple ships above him. Hundreds of purple ships. But then they all *zipped* out of existence, and the sky was black once more.

The endermen were all gone too. Instead there was one solitary figure, walking towards him across the pale yellow ground.

It was either Steve or Herobrine, Dave couldn't tell.

But as the figure got closer he saw that the figure had one normal eye and one white eye.

"Hello, Dave," the figure said, speaking in both Steve and Herobrine's voices at the same time.

Then another figure appeared: a figure with a red t-shirt and white eyes. *Heroprime.*

"You failed once," giggled Heroprime, "and you're going to fail again."

Suddenly The End began to dissolve in front of Dave's eyes: the land, the sky, everything, until there was nothing but white. Endless white.

"Waaa!"

Dave woke up covered in sweat.

"What's wrong now?" mumbled Carl. "I was having a nice dream. I was married to a baked potato and we had little baked potato children, then I ate the children. It was a bit weird, but it was great."

"Nothing," said Dave, "I just had a nightmare."

Dave snuggled down in bed and tried to get back to sleep, but every time he closed his eyes he just saw white...

Endless white...

CHAPTER ONE

The Ruins

Thankfully in the morning it had stopped raining, so Dave, Carl and Spidroth destroyed the house, put the blocks and beds in their rucksacks, then headed further inland.

It was still cold and cloudy, but it felt good not to be wet. They soon found themselves traveling over steep hills covered in tall spruce trees with dark brown trunks. The going was slow, because of the hills, but the trees offered some shelter against the fierce winds coming from the direction of the ocean.

"Hey, what's that weird thing over there?" said Carl.

Dave looked at where Carl was pointing. There was an animal grazing on grass at the foot of one of the hills.

"It's a cow, fool," said Spidroth.

"I dunno," said Carl. "It looks too wooly."

Carl was right, Dave thought. The creature had four legs and was the same shape as a cow, but it was covered in thick orangey-brown wool. It had two small white horns as well.

As Dave looked across the hills he saw other similar creatures grazing on the grass in small groups.

"I'm gonna have a closer look," said Carl.

Carl crept closer to the first creature that they'd spotted, followed by Dave and Spidroth.

Despite their best efforts to be sneaky, the creature saw them coming and turned its head to look at them with the one eye that wasn't covered with wool.

"Mooo," it said.

"Well, it's definitely a cow," said Spidroth. "Some sort of wooly cow."

"Wooly cow," said Carl, "that's a good name for it."

The wooly cow gave them one last bored look, then went back to munching on grass.

"Well," said Carl, as they continued to walk through the hills, "even if we don't discover anything else, at least we can tell the world that we found a new species of cow."

As they came over a particularly large slope, they could see some sort of cobblestone ruins up ahead, nestled between some of the hills.

"It looks like the ruins of a castle," said Dave.

"Great," said Carl. "Let's go around it."

"Don't you want to have a look at it?" Dave asked.

"Not really," said Carl. "Whenever we explore some mysterious building or structure, we always end up running for our lives."

Against Carl's protests, the three of them headed down to take a look at the ruins.

"This place looks ancient," said Spidroth. "It might even date back to the time of the Old People."

Dave had to agree. The building was so old that it was nothing but a few broken cobblestone walls, with no roof and moss growing all over it.

"Do you know much about the Old People?" Dave asked Spidroth.

"She was probably hanging around with them," said Carl. "I know you think she's attractive, Dave, but she's actually an old woman. Be warned."

Dave felt his cheeks glow red.

"I don't think she's... look, just shut up, will you?"

Carl grinned.

"The Old People were long before my time," said Spidroth, ignoring Carl's comments and studying the ruins. "My father always said that they were weak and cowardly, but I don't see how that can be, when they built so many extraordinary things."

"Do you know what happened to them?" Dave asked. "Why they disappeared?"

"Oh yes," said Spidroth. "My father destroyed them."

"What?!" said Dave and Carl together.

"Wait a minute," said Carl, "are you saying that Herobrine destroyed all of the Old People? The people who built the nether fortresses and all that other stuff? How?"

"I don't know," said Spidroth. "He just said that they were gone and that he destroyed them."

"Wow," said Carl. "So we defeated Herobrine when all those Old People couldn't. That means we're more awesome than all the Old People put together."

"*Awesome* is not a word I would use to describe you, creeper," sniffed Spidroth.

"Quiet," said Dave, "I can hear someone coming."

Dave was already wearing his diamond armor, but he quickly

drew his diamond sword. Carl lifted his diamond golem fists, ready to attack, and Spidroth took out her crossbow. As usual, she wasn't wearing any armor.

"Get ready," Dave whispered. "I think there are lots of them!"

Dave's fingers felt sweaty on the grip of his sword. He could hear one of the creatures, whatever they were, moving behind one of the ruined cobblestone walls.

The first thing Dave saw were huge brown horns, sticking around the edge of the wall. He prepared himself, getting ready to strike.

And then the creature walked out from behind the wall. It turned and stared at the three of them, and then said "Baaa!"

"It's... it's a sheep!" said Dave, feeling relieved.

"A weird looking sheep," said Carl. "I've never seen a sheep with horns like that before."

Dave, Carl and Spidroth walked around the side of the ruined wall and saw a whole herd of sheep with large, brown spiral horns. Apart from the horns, they looked just like normal sheep, with white wool and pink faces.

"Well, we've discovered a new species of sheep now too," said Carl. "I think I'm going to call them... horned sheep."

"What a fantastic and original name, " said Spidroth, rolling her eyes. "Anyway, I guess I don't need this crossbow anymore."

Spidroth went to put away her crossbow, but as she did she accidentally brushed the trigger. *TWANG!* A bolt shot out, hitting one of the sheep and instantly *POOF*ing it.

All the other horned sheep turned and looked at them.

"Uh, you don't think they're aggressive do you?" Carl asked. "Normal sheep aren't aggressive."

"They probably don't have those horns for nothing," said Spidroth.

"BAAAA!" roared one of the sheep. Then all the horned sheep lowered their heads and charged.

"Run!" Dave yelled.

"I told you," said Carl. "We always end up running for our lives! Every single time!"

CHAPTER TWO

Phantoms

"I... I think we've lost them," panted Dave.

"Imagine if we'd been killed by sheep," said Carl. "That would have been very embarrassing."

The horned sheep had been much faster than they looked, and there has been a lot of them. Dave, Carl and Spidroth had run for ages, dodging around the old ruins and through trees, but finally they had managed to escape, and were now resting next to a stream.

After a short rest, they kept walking. The land began to flatten out, but it was still quite cloudy overhead.

It was just starting to get dark when Dave spotted a small village up ahead, nestled on the foot of a mountain.

"Wow, so there are people here," said Carl. "I thought it was just gonna be weird cows and sheep."

"We don't know anything about the people in this land," said Spidroth. "It would be wise to keep our distance and observe them first."

Dave agreed.

They made their way towards the village, making sure to keep in the shadow of trees, so that they couldn't be spotted from afar. The sun was almost down now, and Dave was hoping the villagers here were friendly: he really wanted to be able to sleep in a nice warm bed.

"Wait," said Carl, holding out a diamond golem arm to stop Dave and Spidroth.

"What is it?" Dave whispered. "Can you see something?"

"Look up there," said Carl, nodding towards the sky.

Dave looked up. At first he couldn't see anything, but then, when he squinted, he could just make out some winged creatures, really high up.

"Are those bats?" Dave asked.

"I dunno," said Carl. "They're pretty big."

"They're phantoms," said Spidroth.

Carl laughed.

"Phantoms aren't real," he said. "They're just in stories parents tell their kids to make sure that they go to sleep."

Dave had heard the same stories. According to the tales his mum and dad used to tell him, phantoms were vicious flying creatures with huge wings and green eyes who would swoop down and gobble you up if you stayed up too late.

"Phantoms *are* real, creeper," said Spidroth, "but very few people ever see them. They spawn up high, and attack anyone who hasn't slept in over three days. Insomnia attracts them. They feed off tiredness."

"So why are they circling above that village?" Dave asked.

"I assume some fool in that village hasn't been to sleep in over three days," said Spidroth. "Look, there they go! They're attacking!"

She was right: the phantoms were swooping down towards the

town. As they came lower, Dave was amazed at how big they were. At first he'd thought they were around the size of bats, but they were much bigger than that, with massive wingspans and long tails. Their bodies and wings were blue, apart from their white bellies, and their eyes glowed green in the darkness. Their wings left behind a thin trail of gray smoke, which made them seem almost like ghosts. They truly were terrifying creatures.

As they plunged down towards the village, the phantoms began screeching:

"*Ruuuuurk!!*"

"*Hrrrrrrra!!*"

The noises they made were raspy and wheezy, as if their throats were rotten. As they got closer, Dave saw that you could see some of the phantoms' bones through their wings.

"They are undead creatures," said Spidroth. "They can only spawn in the dark, and the sun kills them."

Since the sun had only just gone down, it didn't look like the phantoms would be disappearing anytime soon.

The phantoms had almost reached the village now: they were swooping down towards the wooden buildings at incredible speed.

"We have to help them," said Dave.

"Who, the phantoms?" said Carl.

"No," said Dave, "whoever lives in that village. Those phantoms look like they could rip those houses apart in seconds."

Then, suddenly, a small orange creature climbed up onto the roof of one of the buildings, staring defiantly at the approaching phantoms.

"Is that a cat?" said Carl in disbelief. "That poor little guy's about to get eaten. I'm no fan of cats, but getting eaten by phantoms has gotta be a bad way to go."

But then something extraordinary happened. The phantoms immediately began swooping upwards again, hissing angrily. The orange cat continued to stand his ground, meowing at the phantoms.

"Phantoms are afraid of cats," said Spidroth.

"Wow," said Dave "So that one little guy is defending the village! That's one cool cat!"

The phantoms circled the village for a bit longer, screeching and hissing, but then they flew off, disappearing back into the sky.

"Meow!" the cat said happily.

Once the phantoms were gone, people began to emerge from the houses. But they weren't villagers. In fact, they were unlike any people that Dave had ever seen. Their bodies were normal enough, with two arms and two legs, but their heads... their heads looked like...

"Cows!" said Carl excitedly. "They're cowmen! Real-life cowmen!"

"But cowmen aren't real," said Spidroth in disbelief. "They're just creatures in stories."

"Well they look pretty real to me!" said Carl. "They're just like Master Cowbagio in the *Seth the Elf* comics! Come on, let's go say hi!"

And before Dave could stop him, Carl ran off to speak to the cowmen.

CHAPTER THREE

Cow Village

"Hey!" said Carl, running over to the cowmen. "How are you doing? I'm Carl!"

The cowmen looked terrified, and Dave could hardly blame them. Carl was a creeper wearing the body of a diamond golem. It wasn't something that one saw every day.

"Keep back, monster!" one of the cowmen shouted, brandishing a wooden hoe.

These people aren't warriors, Dave thought, looking at the cowmen. Just like pigmen, they wore no clothes, and none of them had weapons or armor. No wonder they had stayed inside their houses when the phantoms attacked.

"Please," said Dave, running over to join Carl, "we mean you no harm."

"What are you?" a cow-woman asked, giving Dave a strange look. "Your nose... it's so big."

They've never seen a villager before, Dave realized.

"And what kind of beast is that!" another cowman shouted, pointing as Spidroth as she walked over to join Dave and Carl. "A red witch!"

"Call me a witch again and you will face a swift death!" said Spidroth, drawing her diamond sword.

"Spidroth, calm down," said Dave.

"These cow-faced fools need to learn some respect," said Spidroth, reluctantly sheathing her sword. "I may not be the queen I once was, but the Lady Spidrothbrine is still a woman who demands respect."

"I'm Dave," said Dave. "I'm a villager. And this is my friend Carl. He's a creeper."

"He doesn't look like any creeper I've ever seen," said a cowman. "Why's his body made of diamond?"

"He's wearing the body of a diamond golem," said Dave. "But inside that suit he's just a normal creeper."

"Although slightly shorter," said Spidroth.

"Hey!" said Carl.

"And the lady with the red skin is Spidroth," said Dave. "She's a... well, she's a Spidroth."

"Her eyes are white," said a young cowboy. "She looks like a witch."

"That's because I *am* a witch, youngling," said Spidroth. "So you'd better not cross me."

The cowboy gulped.

"We're adventurers," Dave explained to the cowmen. "We're on a quest, but we help people in need when we can. You looked like you were having trouble with those phantoms?"

"Aye, we were," said a cow-woman with broad shoulders, stepping forward. Most of the other cowmen had brown and white hair, but this cow-woman's hair was black and white instead, and she had a gold ring through her nose.

"Are you the leader of the villager?" Dave asked.

"I am," said the black-and-white cowman. "I'm Chief Udder, the chief of Cow Village. It's good to meet you, strangers. I'm sorry if we've been a bit slow to give you a warm welcome, but we don't get many visitors in these parts. A few traders come through from Spectrite City, but that's about it."

She looks tired, Dave thought. In fact, *all* the cowmen looked tired. They looked as if they hadn't slept in days.

"The phantoms," said Dave, "have they been coming often?"

"Aye, those lads come every night," Chief Udder sighed. "If it weren't for ol' Kedi here, our village would be gone by now."

Chief Udder knelt down and stroked the ginger cat, who was rubbing against her legs. Out of the corner of his eye he saw Carl bristle at the sight of the cat. Creepers hated cats, and Carl was no exception.

"Kedi is our only cat," said a cowman. "We'd be finished if anything happened to her. She's the only thing that keeps the phantoms away."

"You bunch of fools!" said Spidroth.

Everyone looked at her.

"If the phantoms keep attacking your village," she said, "then why don't you all just go to sleep?!"

Chief Udder chuckled.

"Because we can't," she said darkly. "We've been cursed."

CHAPTER FOUR

The Curse

"Cursed?" said Dave. "What kind of curse?"

"I'm ashamed to say it, but it is all the fault of my son," said Chief Udder. "There is a witch who lives in the mountains. She has been there for hundreds of years, since my grandfather's grandfather's day. Sometimes she used to come to the village to trade with us or tell stories to the children, and then sometimes she would disappear for years on end, before reappearing again as if nothing had happened. But that all changed a few months ago, when she and my son fell in love."

"A cowman and a witch?" Carl whispered to Dave. "Think about how weird their babies would be."

"Sssh," said Dave.

"My son has always been a wild spirit, but even I was shocked when he came home one day holding hands with the witch. They were in love, he told me. Apparently he had met her while walking in the mountains, and the two of them had fallen for each other. The two of them soon got married, and they built themselves a house in our village to live in. But then, a few weeks later, everything changed. My son, the fool, broke up with the witch. And she was not happy."

"Breaking up with a witch does sound like a very bad idea," said Carl.

"It was," said Chief Udder. "The witch's wrath was terrible to behold. She cursed our village, saying that none of us would ever fall asleep again. And three days after that, the phantom attacks began. There seem to be more of them every night."

"And what about your son?" said Dave.

"He's gone," said Chief Udder.

"Oh no," said Dave. "I'm so sorry."

"Oh, he's still alive," said Chief Udder. "He just left the village. He said he was going to go and plead with the witch to lift the curse, so he took a cat and left to go up the mountain. I wouldn't have minded, but we only had two cats to begin with. So he took fifty per cent of our cats! The lad's an idiot, but he's still my son. I hope he's ok."

"We'll go up the mountain and rescue your son," said Dave. "And we'll try and find the witch too, to get her to release the curse."

"You'd do that for us?" said Chief Udder happily. "But why?"

"Because we're heroes," said Carl. "We kick butts and rescue people. It's what we do. By the way, I don't suppose any of you are ninja masters?"

The cowmen all gave him a blank look.

"You know," said Carl, "like Master Cowbagio in the *Seth the Elf* comics."

"What's Seth the Elf?" asked one cowman.

"What's a comic?" asked another.

Carl shook his head in disgust.

"You don't have comics here? Well, you're in for a treat."

He took two issues of *Seth the Elf* from his rucksack, handing one to a little cow-boy and the other to a little cow-girl.

"Share those around," Carl told them. "A wonderful world of comics awaits you. You don't know what you've been missing."

Since it was still the middle of the night, Chief Udder gave Dave, Carl and Spidroth a house to stay in.

"This was the house my son built for him and the witch to live in after they were married," Chief Udder sighed as she led them in. "They were meant to start a life here, but... well, it didn't work out."

It was a modest wooden house, with a few pictures on the wall, but the most striking thing about it was the purple carpet.

"My son's wife loved purple," said Chief Udder. "I always thought having a purple carpet in a wooden house was a bit much, but it wasn't my place to say anything."

The double bed was purple too.

"Mine!" said Carl, jumping out of his diamond golem suit and landing on the covers. Dave took two regular red beds out of his rucksack and placed them down for him and Spidroth.

"Well Dave," said Spidroth, as she climbed into her bed, "you've volunteered us for yet another quest. How do you ever hope to find this precious ender dragon of yours if you keep going off and getting distracted?"

"We can't abandon people in need," said Dave, climbing into his own bed. "What kind of heroes would we be if we did that?"

"I don't remember ever calling myself a hero," said Spidroth. "Heroes are fools."

"Don't worry, Spidroth," said Carl. "We don't think you're a hero. We just think you're an idiot."

"Alright, settle down you two," said Dave. "We've got a long day ahead of us tomorrow."

Dave's previous experiences with witches had been very mixed. His grandmother was a witch, but he hadn't seen her since he was very young. His memories of her were all happy though, and he remembered her being very kind. The next time he'd met a witch had been a witch named Dotty who'd kidnapped him and his friends and brought them to Herobrine. After that, Dave had been saved by a good witch named Miranda, who claimed that she worked for his grandmother. So Dave knew that witches could be good or bad, but he had no idea what to expect with the witch who they were going to try and find tomorrow. On the one hand, Chief Udder had made her sound very nice, saying the witch read stories to children and traded with the village, but on the other hand she had cursed an entire village in anger, just because her husband had left her.

Dave slept well that night, with no nightmares, and he awoke feeling refreshed. With the sun up, he, Carl and Spidroth were able to have a proper look around the village. The houses were all fairly simple and made of blocks of stripped spruce wood, and to the side of the village was a fenced off field full of horned sheep.

"Aren't those things dangerous?" Dave asked Chief Udder, as they leaned on the fence and looked at the sheep.

"Not if you know how to handle them," said Chief Udder. "They only attack when provoked."

The cowmen gave them some raw mutton for the journey, then Dave, Carl and Spidroth set off up the mountain.

CHAPTER FIVE

The Runaway Husband

At first the journey up the mountain was fairly pleasant. The weather was nice and sunny and the only mobs they saw on the slopes were horned sheep, wooly cows and a few rabbits.

They stopped for lunch by a stream, and Dave cooked some of the mutton.

"Well, horned sheep mutton tastes just the same as regular mutton" said Carl, taking a bite. "It's good, but would go better with a nice potato."

After lunch the slope got steeper. They were walking along the edge of a large ravine when Dave spotted a red creature in the distance.

"Is that a creeper," he asked Carl.

"Uh-oh," said Carl. "Yep, that's a red creeper. Real nasty pieces of work. They explode in a ball of flames and set things on fire. Also they often attack in packs, so keep your eyes peeled."

Thankfully the red creeper was quite far away from them and looking in the other direction, so they made sure to keep their distance from it.

The rest of the day they didn't see any more red creepers, just more horned sheep and woolly cows. As the sun began to go down, a few zombies and skeletons appeared and came over to attack them.

"I'll handle this," said Carl, slamming his diamond fists together.

A skeleton fired its bow at Carl, but the arrow just bounced off of his diamond armor.

"Now's your last chance to scram," Carl told the skeleton.

But the zombies and skeletons were mindless monsters, and just kept trying to attack Carl anyway.

POW! POW! POW! Carl biffed the zombies and skeletons with his fists, sending them flying.

"Good job, Carl," said Dave. "Now let's build some shelter."

But then they heard a voice from nearby:

"Help! Help!"

"Someone needs our help!" said Dave.

"Wow," said Carl, "how can you tell?"

The three of them ran towards the sound of the voice. They came through some trees then saw a cowman up in a tree, surrounded by zombies.

"Help!" the cowman yelled. "Heeeelp me!"

There was something different about this cowman but Dave couldn't put his finger on what it was. And then he realized: the cowmen was wearing clothes. In fact, his clothes, a shirt, trousers and black shoes, looked quite stylish.

Dave, Carl and Spidroth ran over. Three of the zombies turned and tried to grab Dave, but he pulled his diamond sword out and cut them down: SWOOSH, SWOOSH, SWOOSH! Spidroth was jumping around and hacking at the zombies, moving so fast and elegantly that they barely even saw her, and Carl was punching the zombies with his diamond golem fists.

Finally all the zombies had been defeated or had run away. The cowman clambered down the tree.

"Wow, that was incredible," said the cowman. "Thank you so much—I thought my beef was well and truly cooked.

"Creeper face," he said, turning to Carl, "I don't know what the heck you are, but that was some amazing stuff. And that diamond body... I've got to get me one of those!"

"Are you Chief Udder's son?" Dave asked.

"Guilty as charged," said the cowman. "The name's Jean-Cowphio. One part cow, one part handsome, and ten parts awesome fashion sense."

"I'm Dave," said Dave. "Pleased to meet you."

"Dave," said Jean-Cowphio thoughtfully, "no, you don't look like a Dave. I think I'm going to call you... D-Dog. How'd you like your new name, D-Dog?"

"Um..." said Dave, not knowing what to say.

"And who is this?" said Jean-Cowphio, taking Spidroth's hand. "My lady, I am in love! Come on, let's get married right now."

Spidroth snatched her hand away.

"We've heard that you already have a wife," she said.

"Well, technically," shrugged Jean-Cowphio. "But things didn't work out. If you've met my mum, I assume you know about the curse?"

"We do," said Dave. "Apparently your wife didn't take your break up very well."

"Yeah, she had it bad for me," said Jean-Cowphio. "What can I say—when the ladies fall for Jean-Cowphio, they fall for him bad."

"How long were you married?" Dave asked.

"One week," said Jean-Cowphio.

"One week?!" exclaimed Carl. "You broke off your marriage after only one week?!"

"Hey, I'm an impulsive guy," said Jean-Cowphio. "I fell in love, I wasn't thinking straight. When I proposed, I never expected Vee would say yes. But she did, and we got married. I thought I could make it work, but the J-Meister can't be tied down to one woman."

"The J-Meister... that's you?" said Carl.

"Yeah, that's what I call myself sometimes," said Jean-Cowphio. "I'm normally better with nicknames but I haven't slept in a few weeks, thanks to the curse."

"So what's your plan?" Carl asked. "We heard you went up the mountain to find the witch and apologize?"

"Well, that's what I told my mum," said Jean-Cowphio. "Really I came up here to get away from her nagging. She wouldn't stop blaming me for the curse on the village."

"Well it was all your fault," said Carl.

"Technically yes," said Jean-Cowphio. "Anyway, I built myself a sweet crib up here, and I've been chilling on the mountain ever since. It was all going great until this morning, when my cat ran away. I need to get her back, as she's the only thing keeping me safe from the phantoms. Talking of which..."

Jean-Cowphio looked up. Dave followed his gaze and saw that the sky above them was full of circling phantoms.

"How far is your house?" Dave asked.

"I dunno, D-Dog," said Jean-Cowphio. "I kind of got lost."

"*Ruuuuurk!!*" one of the phantoms screeched, and they all

32

began swooping down towards the ground.

"Battle stations!" yelled Dave.

"Aw man," grinned Jean-Cowphio, "you guys are so cool! Look at you, posing with your weapons, getting ready to fight! You guys rock!"

"Just keep out of our way," grunted Carl.

"No problemo," said Jean-Cowphio. "I'm just gonna stand back and watch you guys do your thing."

Dave had put away his sword and taken out his bow. Spidroth had her crossbow, and Carl, as always, had his diamond golem suit. Jean-Cowphio was just leaning against a tree, watching them with a big grin on his face.

"Oh man," said Jean-Cowphio, "this battle is going to be SWEET!"

CHAPTER SIX

Attack of the Phantoms

"Hrrrrrrrra!!" a phantom screeched, flying straight at Dave.

Up close, the phantoms were far larger than Dave had thought they were, and quicker too. The phantom swooped towards Dave, its green eyes glowing and its teeth bared.

TWANG! Dave fired an arrow right between the phantom's eyes, and *POOF,* it disappeared in a puff of smoke. But then two more phantoms were swooping towards him. Dave jumped out of the way and landed on the ground. He didn't have time to string his bow again, so he dropped it and pulled out his diamond sword.

"Ruuuuur!" hissed one of the phantoms.

SWOOSH! Dave swung his diamond sword and cut both the phantoms down. *POOF, POOF!*

Dave jumped back to his feet. Carl and Spidroth were fighting off the phantoms too. Spidroth was running around, firing at them with her bow, but Carl was really struggling. The phantoms were clinging to his golem suit, biting it with their fangs as he struggled to get them off. Some of the phantoms were clinging to his back, and he couldn't reach round and remove them.

Dave ran forward to help Carl, but then a phantom smashed into him from the side, and he fell to the floor, dropping his sword. The phantom was on top of him, trying to bite his face, and Dave desperately tried to keep it at bay with his hands.

"Hrra hrrra!" the phantom hissed as it snapped its teeth at Dave's face. It was heavier than Dave would have thought, and Dave couldn't push it off him.

Then, suddenly, a diamond blade appeared through the middle of the phantom's chest.

"Ruur?" said the phantom. Then *POOF*, it was gone. Jean-Cowphio was standing behind it, clutching Dave's sword, a nervous look on his face.

"Hey!" said Jean-Cowphio excitedly. "I did something!"

Dave got to his feet and picked up his bow. Carl was still struggling with the phantoms. The creeper had retreated inside his golem armor like a turtle hiding in its shell, to stop them biting his face.

"Come on," Dave said to Jean-Cowphio, "let's help Carl."

They both ran over. Dave started firing arrows at the phantoms on Carl's back, and Jean-Cowphio started swinging the diamond sword at any phantoms that swooped near them. It was pretty clear that Jean-Cowphio had never used a sword before, but he was managing to hold his own.

"You phantoms want a fight? You've got one!" Jean-Cowphio yelled. "Courtesy of the one, the only, Jean-Cowphio!"

Now the phantoms were no longer clinging to him, Carl stuck his head back out of his diamond golem armor.

"Thanks," he said to Dave.

Spidroth was still holding her own as well, firing arrows at the phantoms and dodging out of the way before they could attack her.

"Die, fools!" she was yelling. "Feel the wrath of Spidroth!"

"Dang, that red woman is awesome!" Jean-Cowphio said to Dave. "Does she have a boyfriend? Because this guy right here is definitely interested."

"Aren't you still married?" said Dave.

"Technically," said Jean-Cowphio. "But a guy like me can't be pinned down. I'm a free spirit. There's too much of the J-Meister to go around."

Some more phantoms swooped towards them. WHAM! Carl biffed some of them, sending them flying. Jean-Cowphio managed to hit a couple of them with the diamond sword and Dave fired at the others with his bow.

Soon all the phantoms were defeated, leaving nothing but bits of white slimy skin behind.

"Phantom membranes," said Jean-Cowphio, picking one of them up. "Pretty gross, but apparently you can use them in potions or whatever."

Dave picked some of the phantom membranes up and put them in his rucksack. He liked to pick up all the weird things he found on his adventure, in case they became useful later, even though it did make his rucksack very heavy.

"Yo D-Dog, have you ever thought about using an ender chest to store some of that stuff?" Jean-Cowphio asked. "That rucksack looks HEAV-EE!"

Dave had heard of ender chests, but he'd never really given them much thought. Apparently if you put items in one ender chest, you'd be able to access them in any other ender chest in the world, no matter how far away they were.

"Meow!"

Suddenly a black cat came running towards them through the trees. Carl jumped out the way of the cat, a look of terror on his face, and it ran up on Jean-Cowphio and rubbed against his legs.

"Mr Whiskers!" said Jean-Cowphio excitedly, picking up the cat. "Where did you go, little dude?"

"Meow," said Mr Whiskers.

"Come on," Jean-Cowphio said to Dave and the others, "I think I remember which way my crib is now. So get your best shoes on, and let's get walking!"

CHAPTER SEVEN

The Crib

From the outside, Jean-Cowphio's "crib" was just a normal-looking wooden shack, but inside was a different story.

"Wow," said Carl, as they walked inside. "I wasn't expecting this."

The floor of the shack was covered in red carpet, the walls were covered in paintings, and the room was lit by a redstone lamp hanging from the ceiling. There was one bed, which had yellow covers, and in the corner of the room was a jukebox, a crafting table and an ender chest.

"I'm afraid I'm low on seats, but please sit on the bed," said Jean-Cowphio. "And D-Dog, let me show you the wonders of ender chests."

Jean-Cowphio led Dave over to the ender chest.

"How do you build ender chests, anyway?" Dave asked, looking at the chest. It was green, but such a dark green that it was almost black, and there was a mark on the front of it that reminded Dave of an eye of ender."

"No idea, dude," said Jean-Cowphio. "When my tribe first

founded our village, back in my grand-daddy's grand-daddy's day, they just found a few of these chests among some nearby ruins. I think the Ancients must have used them."

"The Ancients?" said Dave.

"You know," said Jean-Cowphio, "the old dudes who used to live here a zillion years ago."

"Oh yeah," said Dave. "We call them the Old People."

"That's a pretty dumb name," said Jean-Cowphio. "But each to their own, I guess. Now come on, let me show you how awesome this baby is. Open it up and have a look inside."

Dave lifted the golden clasp at the front of the chest and then opened the lid.

"It's empty," he said to Jean-Cowphio.

"Oh really?" said Jean-Cowphio, grinning. The cowman closed the lid, then opened the chest again and pulled out a pair of gold boots.

"My golden booties," said Jean-Cowphio. "That's the beauty of ender chests—only you can get your stuff out of them! Plus they look really cool."

Looking at the ender chest, Dave had a sudden flash of inspiration. The light green mark on the chest didn't just look like an eye of ender, Dave was pretty sure it *was* an eye of ender. And the smooth, dark green surface of the chest felt remarkably similar to obsidian.

"Can I use your crafting table for a second?" Dave asked Jean-Cowphio.

"Dave, baby, it would be my pleasure," said the cowman.

Dave went over to the crafting table. Jean-Cowphio, Carl and Spidroth all gathered around him.

"What you up to?" Carl asked him.

"Just trying out a theory," said Dave.

Dave took out an eye of ender from his bag and placed it in the middle square of the crafting table. Then he placed eight tiny obsidian blocks in the squares around it. For a second, nothing happened, then *POP*—a tiny ender chest appeared in the middle of the table.

"Wooooow," said Jean-Cowphio. "D-Dog, you did it! What's that crazy green eye thing you used?"

"I can't tell you, sorry," said Dave.

Ever since he'd learned how much Herobrine wanted to go to The End, Dave had told the secret of the eyes of ender to as few people as possible. Dave had read about eyes of ender in a really old book he'd found in an ancient stronghold below his village, and, as far as he knew, very few people knew about them and their secret: that they could lead people to The End. Even Herobrine seemed to have no idea about eyes of ender, and Steve hadn't known either, until Alex had told him.

"Ok you keep your secrets," said Jean-Cowphio. "You're one mysterious guy, D-Dog, you and your band of traveling dudes, just roaming about the place beating up bad guys. Does your crew have a name?"

"A name?" said Dave. "Er, no."

"Then let the J-Meister give you one," said Jean-Cowphio. "Let's see, how about... The Three Dudes!"

"I'm not a 'dude'," said Spidroth, giving Jean-Cowphio an angry look.

"Hey gorgeous, girls can be dudes too," said Jean-Cowphio. "Being a dude is a state of mind. But ok, if you don't like that one, how about, The Battle Dudes!"

"Listen," said Dave, seeing the angry look on Spidroth's face, "let's move on from the team-name thing, shall we? We told your mum that we'd help to lift the witch's curse. Do you want to come with us?"

"I dunno," said Jean-Cowphio, "Vee can get very angry with me sometimes. The last time I saw her she was not a happy camper."

"Well, you did break off your marriage to her after only one week," said Carl.

"So the witch's name is Vee?" asked Dave.

"Yeah," said Jean-Cowphio. "Although I sometimes call her my little Veevee. She's a beautiful woman. The love of my life."

"The love of your life?" said Spidroth angrily. "Then why did you break up with her?"

"I'm a complicated guy," shrugged Jean-Cowphio. "My mind is firing like a redstone circuit, *pew, pew, pew!* Too many thoughts! Too many ideas! And it's even worse now that I can't sleep, my mind is racing all the time!"

"Well," said Dave, "you may not be able to sleep, but I think Carl, Spidroth and I need to."

Jean-Cowphio seemed nice enough to Dave, but he was exhausting to talk to. He didn't seem to have an off switch.

"No problemo," said Jean-Cowphio. "Just put some beds down wherever you want. I'll be outside, practicing my rhymes."

And Jean-Cowphio left, leaving Dave, Carl and Spidroth alone.

"He's a bit much, isn't he?" said Dave.

"He's an idiot," said Carl.

"For once I agree with the creeper," said Spidroth.

Dave took three beds out of his backpack and placed them

down. It was a bit of a tight squeeze, but he managed to make them all fit.

Dave snuggled up under his covers. He was just about to get to sleep when he heard some rapping coming from somewhere outside:

"Yo it's Jean-Cowphio and my rhymes are hot,

"Serve them up to your gran, put them in a teapot.

"If you think your beats are better, I'm here to tell you that they're not,

"Now you've heard my words, and baby, baby that's your lot."

"Idiot," muttered Carl sleepily.

CHAPTER EIGHT

The Journey up the Mountain

When Dave woke up the next morning and went outside, Jean-Cowphio was sitting on a tree stump nearby, still rapping. The cowman had enough sense to surround himself with torches, Dave was pleased to see, so no hostile mobs had attacked him.

"Yo D-Dog!" Jean-Cowphio said. "Wanna hear a sick rhyme? This one's so sick it needs a healing potion."

"Maybe later," said Dave. "Can you tell me where the witch lives? We're going to go further up the mountain today."

"She lives right at the top," said Jean-Cowphio. "She's got a little cave there. I say little, but it is one fine crib. We're talking plush purple carpet, gold block walls, fancy bookshelves. I mean, I'm not much of a book guy, but I can appreciate a good, color-coordinated shelf. She has these awesome colored chest things too to store all her stuff, I think she calls them shulker boxes. And this awesome table: it's like obsidian, but it has this floating book on the top of it, and weird symbols flow from the bookshelves around it, into the floating book. I'm not explaining it very well, but it's so cool. She's got so much cool stuff."

Dave knew that Jean-Cowphio was talking about: it was an enchanting table. It made sense that a witch had one, to enchant items with magic.

Suddenly Dave found himself thinking about the witch. What exactly was his plan? Was he just going to try and convince the witch to lift the curse? And if she refused was he going to attack her? That might not go so well: if she was powerful enough to curse an entire town, she must be pretty strong.

No, Dave realized, there was only one plan that would work: they had to patch things up between the witch and Jean-Cowphio. Even if they didn't stay married, if Jean-Cowphio could apologize properly, maybe the witch would lift the curse?

"Jean-Cowphio," Dave said to the cowman, "will you come with us? I know your people have managed to keep the phantoms at bay with that cat they have, but it's only a matter of time before someone gets hurt. Or worse. We need to convince the witch to lift the curse."

Jean-Cowphio sighed.

"You want me to face Vee again?" he said. "I dunno if that's a good idea. She's got it in for yours truly. She hates me more than creepers hate ocelots. She hates me more than all the other cowmen in my village hate wearing clothes."

"Even so, you may be our only hope," said Dave. "From what I've been told, it seems like this witch used to be reasonable and nice. We need to try and convince her to be reasonable and nice again."

"She was nice," sighed Jean-Cowphio. "I guess I can't blame her for falling in love with me. Ok, I'll come with you guys. But if we're going to be questing, I'll need some armor. You got any spare?"

"I think I've got another full set of diamond armor in my bag," said Dave.

"No way, man," said Jean-Cowphio. "Diamonds are so last season. I want GO-OLD. Gold, baby. Solid gold armor. I've already got the booties, but I need the full set. I need that bling, baby. The J-Meister needs his gold."

"You know, gold armor isn't really all that great," said Dave. "It breaks pretty easily."

But Jean-Cowphio wouldn't listen, and insisted on gold. Dave had quite a few gold blocks in his bag, so he built Jean-Cowphio a full set of armor, minus the gold boots, which the cowman already had.

While looking through his rucksack, Dave also took the opportunity to empty some of his stuff into the ender chest in Jean-Cowphio's house. He had so many cobblestone blocks and iron ingots, as well as loads of wood and other assorted blocks. Dave emptied a lot of it into the ender chest, and his rucksack felt so much lighter. He still had the little ender chest that he'd made the day before, so he knew he could access all his old stuff if he needed to.

When Carl and Spidroth got up, Dave cooked them all some mutton for breakfast.

"What the heck are you wearing?" Carl asked Jean-Cowphio, who was already kitted out in his gold armor.

"This is my BL-ING!" said Jean-Cowphio happily. "My boy Dave was good enough to kit the J-Meister out. Solid gold from head to toe, baby! Bring on the zombies! Bring on the skeletons! Bring on those weird green cube things you get in swamps!"

"Slimes?" said Dave.

"Those are the ones!" said Jean-Cowphio. "I love those things. I'd love to squish one of them with my hands. They're so squelchy and gross and awesome."

So the four of them headed off up the mountain. Before long the air began to grow thinner. Dave looked around and saw that they were very high up: he could see the tiny wooden houses of Cow Villager far below, the hills that he, Carl and Spidroth had first seen the wooly cows in, and the ocean beyond that. There were more ruins too, and the legs and torso of a huge statue, rising up in the middle of a forest. The statue's head and both its arms were missing.

"What's that statue?" Dave asked Jean-Cowphio.

"Oh, it's just more stuff the Ancients left behind," said Jean-Cowphio. "There are so many ruins around here, I guess this must have been one of their cities or whatever. My mum is fascinated with all that stuff, but I've no idea why. Old stuff is boooooooring."

Dave had seen plenty of old statues before on his quest, most of them being statues of Steve. The headless statue could have been of Steve once, but it was impossible to tell now. Dave hadn't thought about Steve in a long time. He hoped he was doing ok, wherever he was. Steve had headed west in a boat that Dave and his friends had been hoping to take, so if he'd succeeded in crossing the ocean he had to be somewhere in this strange land they'd come to. Just like Dave, Steve was on a quest to find and slay the ender dragon, and Dave's worst nightmare was that Steve would find the dragon first. Steve had a big head start on Dave, but thankfully for Dave, Steve was easily distracted and often forgot things. With any luck, Steve would have forgotten about the dragon by now. At least that's what

Dave hoped.

The higher up the mountain they got, the less trees there were. The ground was mostly stone now, and the going was tough. They still came across the occasional horned sheep, but there were no more wooly cows.

When they stopped for lunch, Dave cooked mutton for him, Spidroth and Jean-Cowphio and a baked potato for Carl. They were running low on potatoes, so Carl said that no-one else was allowed to have one.

Dave had just packed up the campfire he'd used to cook their food, when Carl came rushing over.

"Look up there," Carl whispered.

They all looked up the mountain, following Carl's gaze. At first Dave couldn't see what Carl was talking about, but then he saw them: lots of red creatures on the slopes above them.

Red creepers.

"Uh-oh," said Jean-Cowphio. "Those guys are bad news. The last time I was up here I had Vee to protect me. The red creepers knew better than to attack her. But I don't think we'll be so lucky."

"Why are there so many of them?" Dave asked. "Do they like it high up?"

"They have a nest up here," said Jean-Cowphio. "I've never seen it, but apparently there's a creeper queen who lives up here, and these are all her kids."

"Aw man," said Carl, "red creeper queens are the worst."

"Well, we've faced creeper queens in the past," said Dave, thinking back to the blue creeper queen back in the mountains around Villagertropolis.

"That was a *blue* creeper queen," said Carl. "Red ones are ten times worse. Or so my uncles always told me."

"Well let's try and avoid them as best we can," said Dave. "The last thing we want on these steep slopes is a battle."

All it would take up here would be one misstep and they would suffer a nasty fall, Dave knew. There were cliffs and sharp falls everywhere. Fighting a load of creepers would not be a good idea.

"Don't worry too much about creepers," said Jean Cowphio, "we've got Mr Whiskers!"

And he picked the black cat up and held it in front of Carl's face.

"Get that evil thing away from me!" said Carl.

"You see?" grinned Jean Cowphio. "Creepers hate these guys."

"How can you still be afraid of a cat when you're wearing a huge suit of diamond golem armor?" Dave asked Carl.

"Cats are evil," said Carl. "They can't be trusted."

Soon the steep, stony slopes of the mountain were so bare, with so few trees, that it was impossible for them to stay hidden from the red creepers.

"Jean Cowphio, you and Mr Whiskers should walk at the front," said Dave. "We can't hide from the red creepers, but hopefully the sight of a cat will keep them at bay. Spidroth and I will have our bows ready, just in case any of them come too near."

Jean Cowphio was a bit nervous about walking in front, but he agreed.

Dave's plan seemed to work. As Dave and the others made their way up the slopes, the red creepers kept their distance, just staring at them with their angry black eyes.

As long as we've got the cat, we should be alright, thought Dave. According to Jean Cowphio, the witch lived right at the top of the mountain, and from the look of it, Dave thought that they should be able to get there before sundown. He didn't like the idea of spending the night on the mountain surrounded by red creepers—cat or no cat.

Just then, something small and white ran past them, shaking Dave from his thoughts.

"What was that?" said Dave.

"I think it was a rabbit," said Spidroth.

Suddenly Mr Whiskers ran off down the mountain, chasing after the rabbit.

"Mr Whiskers!" yelled Jean Cowphio. "Come back, my boy!"

But the cat was gone.

"Uh-oh," said Dave, looking around at the red creepers, who were all starting to slither towards them, "we're in big trouble."

"Hey D-Dog, I don't like all this negativity," said Jean Cowphio. "Come on my dude, whatever's put that frown on your face, it can't be that bad."

"We're about to be blown to bits by red creepers," said Dave.

"Oh yeah," said Jean Cowphio. "I guess that is pretty bad."

CHAPTER NINE

The Red Creepers Attack

"Stay back or we'll have to shoot!" Dave yelled at the creepers. But they didn't take any notice, they just kept slithering towards them.

"Can you use a bow?" Dave asked Jean-Cowphio.

"Can I?" said Jean-Cowphio. "You're asking me, Jean 'J-Meister' Cowphio, if I can use a bow?"

"Yes," said Dave.

"No," said Jean-Cowphio. "I can't."

Dave reached into his bag and pulled out a spare crossbow.

"This is a crossbow," Dave told Jean-Cowphio, "you just point and pull the trigger. You load the arrows in there."

"Niiice," said Jean-Cowphio, taking the crossbow.

The creepers were within arrow range now.

"Shall we shoot?" Spidroth asked Dave.

"This is your last chance!" Dave yelled at the creepers. "Stay back!"

But the creepers ignored him.

"Ok," said Dave, "attack!"

TWANG! TWANG! TWANG! Spidroth started firing her

crossbow, Dave started firing his regular bow, and Jean-Cowphio even managed to join in, once he got the hang of the crossbow. Carl was blasting the creepers too, using the arm cannon that Professor Hector had fitted to his suit, back on PVP Island.

"Yeah boy!" said Jean-Cowphio. "This crossbow thing is pretty fun!"

The red creepers were tough, and it took Dave three arrows to take each one down. Once the third arrow hit the creepers they'd fall over and go *POOF*, but for every creeper Dave slew, there were two more to take its place.

Dave was firing arrows as fast as his fingers could move, but there were just too many red creepers. Thankfully none of them had been able to get close enough to explode yet, but it was only a matter of time.

"Right, I think it's time for some bashing," said Carl. He transformed his arm cannon back into a fist then rushed into the crowd of creepers, swinging his huge diamond arms and sending them flying.

Carl was fighting the creepers off quickly, but he didn't notice one of them slither up behind him.

"Watch out, Carl!" Dave yelled.

FWOOOOM!!!! The creeper exploded in a massive ball of flames. Thankfully Carl was protected from the fire by his diamond suit, but the force of the explosion made him topple over, and he began rolling down the mountain.

"Waaaaaaaaaa!" Carl yelled.

Then *SLAM*, Carl smashed into a tree and stopped rolling.

Dave wanted to go and help his friend, but he, Spidroth and Jean-Cowphio were still surrounded by endless red creepers. The creepers were so close now that Dave switched to his diamond sword, and began cutting the creepers down with his blade, trying to do it quickly before they exploded.

All Dave could here was H*ISS, HISS, HIIIIIIIIS,* as the creepers closed in around them. They were fighting a losing battle, and unlike Carl they didn't have diamond golem suits to protect them from the fire if the creepers exploded.

We've got to escape, Dave knew. But they were surrounded on all sides, where could they escape to?

And then Dave knew what he had to do. It was a dumb idea, but it was the only idea he had.

"Get close to me!" Dave yelled to Spidroth and Jean-Cowphio. They did as he said, then Dave put away his sword and pulled out a diamond pickaxe.

"What fool plan is this?" said Spidroth.

"Trust me," said Dave, and he began digging straight down.

Chunk, chunk chunk! Dave dug down with his pickaxe, going through stone block after stone block. Since Spidroth and Jean-Cowphio had been standing on the same block as him, they were going down with him too, into a one-block pit that was getting deeper and deeper every second.

"Fool, do you have any idea how dangerous it is to dig straight down?" Spidroth demanded. "I never took you for a noob."

"It was either this or get fried by those creepers," said Dave. "Talking of which..."

The small square of light above them suddenly went dark, and Dave saw the silhouette of a creeper appear, looking down at them.

And then it began to rain creepers: the red creepers were jumping down into the hole!

"Shoot them!" Dave yelled.

Dave kept digging down with his pickaxe and Spidroth and Jean-Cowphio aimed their bows upwards and shot the creepers as they fell.

"Is every day for you guys this crazy?!" said Jean-Cowphio.

It was a tight squeeze in the tunnel, with three of them all crammed together, but Dave still managed to keep digging down, as Spidroth and Jean-Cowphio continued to shoot. Gunpowder was showering down on them from the slain creepers. Dave would have loved to have picked it up and put it in his rucksack, but he didn't have time.

Please don't let us fall into lava, Dave prayed. He still remembered the first time he'd ever dug straight down: it had been on the first night of his adventure and he'd been trying to escape a group of zombies. He'd dug straight down into a lake of lava but had thankfully landed on a small bit of land in the middle of the lake. He'd been lucky that time, but Dave knew that his luck had to run out eventually. He just hoped that this wasn't the time it did.

Then, suddenly, Dave dug through a stone block and found himself falling. Thankfully it wasn't into lava and it wasn't very far: he, Spidroth and Jean-Cowphio fell a few blocks down and landed on hard ground. It was completely dark, so Dave reached into his bag, pulled out a torch and placed it down.

They were inside a narrow cave passage. Most of the walls were stone, with a few deposits of coal and lapis lazuli in the walls.

"Ooo," said Jean-Cowphio, looking at a block of lapis lazuli ore, "they gots the diamonds down here! D to the I to the A to the—"

"We haven't got time for this," said Dave, grabbing the cowman by the arm. "Come on!"

The three of them ran off through the cave, Dave placing down torches as they went to light their way. Behind them some more red creepers fell through the hole Dave had dug, exploding into flames as they hit the ground.

"Those red creepers are CRAY-ZEE," said Jean-Cowphio, looking back.

"What are we going to do about Carl?" Spidroth asked Dave. "I'd be happy to leave him for dead, of course, but I know he's your friend."

"We've got to find a way up and rescue him," said Dave. "Hopefully he'll be ok until we get there."

Dave felt guilty about leaving Carl behind, but he'd had no choice. If he, Spidroth and Jean-Cowphio hadn't made their escape when they had, the three of them would have been fried by the red creepers.

There has to be a way up to the surface somewhere, thought Dave, as they came around another corner in the cave. He could dig back up to the surface, but he knew that would take too long.

They ran around another corner, but suddenly came face-to-face with hundreds of red creepers, all slithering towards them.

"Run!" Dave yelled.

They ran back the way they'd come, but then Dave saw, to his horror, that there were red creepers coming around a corner that way as well.

They were trapped: with red creepers closing in from both sides.

"The J-Meister likes to put a positive spin on things, but this is looking bad," said Jean-Cowphio. "We're gonna get cooked like porkchops. Extra crispy."

"We'll have to dig up to the surface," said Dave, reaching into his bag and getting pickaxes for Spidroth and Jean-Cowphio.

"The Lady Spidrothbrine does not dig," said Spidroth.

"Well she's going to have to start," said Dave. "Come on!"

Dave began hacking at the stone wall of the cave with his pickaxe. A moment later, Spidroth and Jean-Cowphio joined him, all three of them digging diagonally upwards. Dave looked around and saw that the creepers were closing in on them.

If we can just dig a little further, we can block the passage behind us with obsidian, Dave thought. *It'll take those creepers a while to get through that.*

But then Dave dug upwards into another cave passageway, and all the hope drained from him. This new cave passageway was packed full of red creepers, who all started rushing towards them.

They had nowhere to go. There were creepers in front of them, and creepers coming up behind them, up the slope they'd dug.

"Get your weapons ready," said Dave. "If we're going to go, let's go out fighting."

But then, to Dave's surprise, the creepers didn't come any closer.

"What are they doing?" Jean-Cowphio whispered.

Then the creepers in front of them moved to the side, creating a passageway.

"I think they want us to go that way," said Dave.

"We shouldn't do it," said Spidroth. "Can we trust them?"

"I don't think we've got much choice," said Dave.

CHAPTER TEN

The Cavern

The red creepers led Dave, Spidroth and Jean-Cowphio through the caves. Dave kept looking around, searching for an escape route, but there wasn't one. They were surrounded by a huge crowd of creatures that could explode into flames at any minute. And if one creeper exploded, they were so packed together that there would probably be a chain reaction and they'd all explode. There were so many of them that it would probably blow a hole in the side of the mountain.

How are we going to get out of this? Dave thought desperately. He wondered if they could maybe use the Dimensional Portal Device to escape to the mirror universe, but it was in his rucksack, and he was unlikely to be able to get the device out, turn it on and get Spidroth, Jean-Cowphio and himself through the portal before the red creepers blew them to bits.

No, for now they would have to keep going where the creepers were leading them. Dave didn't see what choice they had.

The creepers seemed to be bringing them deeper into the mountain; the passageways they were being taken down were gradually sloping downwards.

"Well, at least I won't have to deal with those phantom dudes tonight," said Jean-Cowphio sadly. "I'll get to be eaten by a creeper queen instead. That is not the way J-Diggidy thought he was going to go out."

"The creeper queen?" said Dave. "Is that where you think they're taking us?"

"No doubt," said Jean-Cowphio. "Vee told me that the creepers sometimes bring their prey into the mountain to feed their queen. I guess even creeper queens gotta eat."

Soon the dark tunnels they were walking through began to get brighter, lit by a deep orange light from somewhere up ahead.

That's the glow of lava, Dave knew. He'd seen it enough times before.

It was getting warmer too. It was so hot and muggy that Dave started sweating and his throat became dry.

Finally, after walking for what seemed like hours, the creepers led them into a gigantic cavern. In the middle of the cavern was a lake of lava.

Where's the queen? Dave wondered. He looked all around the cave, but could see no sign of a creeper queen. There were clutches of red eggs stuck to the walls in clumps with slimy liquid, but no sign of whatever had laid them.

Some red creepers were already gathered by the edge of the lava lake, and Dave was surprised to see that one of them was green: it was Carl! The diamond golem suit was being worn by one of the red creepers, its red head sticking out the top as it stood guard over Carl.

"Hey Carl," said Dave, as he, Spidroth and Jean-Cowphio were led down to join the other group of creepers by the side of the lake.

"Oh no," said Carl. "I was hoping you idiots were going to rescue me."

"What happened?" Dave asked him.

"When I fell down the mountain I smacked into a tree and got knocked out," said Carl. "When I woke up, these red idiots had stolen my suit and were carrying me into the caves."

"HISSSSSS," said the red creeper in the diamond golem suit.

"Yeah, you heard me," said Carl. "You're idiots."

"Stop babbling, fools," whispered Spidroth. "How are we going to get out of here?"

"Look up there," whispered Carl, pointing with his head.

Dave looked. Up in one of the corners of the cavern was a small hole where they could see daylight. It looked like the sun was starting to go down, as the light was orange.

"And how are we meant to get up there, fool?" Spidroth demanded.

"I dunno," said Carl. "Dave's the guy with the plans normally."

Suddenly there was bubbling from the middle of the lava lake.

"Uh oh," said Carl. "This doesn't look good."

The creepers all began to hiss in unison: it was almost like they were chanting.

HISS HISS! HISS HISS HIIIIIIIS!

Then *FWOOOOOOSH,* something huge rose from the lava lake. Then *FWOOOOOOSH*, a second thing rose from the lake, and *FWOOOOOOSH*, a third thing rose from the lake.

And Dave found himself looking up in horror at a three-headed monster: three long red necks with gigantic red creeper heads on the end of them.

"Whoa Nelly!" gasped Jean-Cowphio. "It's a three-headed creeper!"

"Correction," said Carl, "it's a creeper *queen*."

CHAPTER ELEVEN
The Queen

The red creeper queen looked nothing like the blue creeper queen that Dave had seen before. He guessed that different creeper species must have different types of queens, but right now he had more important things to worry about.

The red creeper queen's three heads were looking down at them, with orange goo dripping from each of her mouths.

That's lava, Dave realized.

KRRRRIIIIIIIIIIIIIIIIIIII!!!!!!!!!!!!!

Suddenly the three creeper queen heads screeched, then each other mouths fired out a jet of lava, hitting the cavern wall. Dave looked around and saw that the lava was so hot that it boiled a hole in the stone walls of the cavern.

"Ok, three heads and it can breathe lava?!" said Jean-Cowphio. "Jean-Cowphio is checking out. This is too much for me. Give me back to the phantoms, baby! I miss the phantoms!"

Suddenly Dave had an idea.

"Jean-Cowphio," Dave whispered.

"You got him right here," said Jean-Cowphio. "The J-Meister

at your service."

"I need you to get up to that hole in the cavern wall," Dave said, pointing up at the tiny gap in the cavern roof. "Once you're there, I need you to open up that gap and let the phantoms in. The sun's going down and they're going to be hunting you again. We need to bring them in here, and hopefully they'll attack the creeper queen."

"D-Dog, that's a good idea, but I can see two problemos," said Jean-Cowphio. "One, how am I going to get up there? And two, how am I going to get over there without all these red creeper jerks blowing me to bits? Or the creeper queen eating me?"

"Use these blocks," Dave said, reaching into backpack and handing Jean-Cowphio a handful of assorted blocks. "Jump up, lay one below your feet, then do it again and again, building yourself a tower up to the hole, and then use my pickaxe to make it wider and get the phantoms in here. Carl, Spidroth and I will give you a distraction."

"Ok daddy-o," said Jean-Cowphio. "You got it."

The red creepers began pushing and shoving Dave and the others, moving them closer to the lava lake, where the creeper queen's three huge heads were waiting for them.

"Spidroth, Carl, get ready to attack when I say," whispered Dave.

"I don't have my suit," Carl whispered back.

"Don't worry," said Dave. "I'll get it for you. NOW!"

Dave and Spidroth immediately sprung into action. Dave turned around, while at the same time reaching into his backpack. He pulled out a crossbow and *TWANG*, fired an arrow right at the red creeper who was wearing Carl's diamond golem armor. The creeper went *POOF* and the armor collapsed. Carl quickly slithered inside.

While this was happening, Spidroth began swinging her diamond sword around, *POOF*ing the red creepers. But there were so many of them that she couldn't get them all, and some of them began to HISS.

"Watch out!" Carl roared. He was wearing his diamond golem suit again now, and he ran over, using his diamond body to shield Dave and Spidroth as the red creepers began to explode.

"SKRRRRRRIIIIIII!!!!!"

Above them, the three huge heads of the red creeper queen screamed in anger, looking down at the chaos below.

One of the creeper queen's heads unleashed a torrent of lava from its mouth, right towards Dave, Carl and Spidroth. Thankfully Carl acted fast, grabbing Dave under one arm and Spidroth under the other, and jumping out of the way. The red creepers they left behind weren't so lucky though, and were drenched in lava.

While lava was spraying and red creepers were exploding in flames, Dave looked over and saw that Jean-Cowphio was doing his job too: he'd used the distraction to run over to where the hole in the cavern ceiling was, and he'd started building his tower up to it, using the blocks that Dave had given him: jumping up and placing blocks underneath his feet over and over again. The sky outside was black now, and Dave knew that the phantoms must be circling overhead.

Dave, Carl and Spidroth kept fighting off the red creepers: Dave and Spidroth with swords and Carl using his fists and his arm cannon. Another of the huge creeper queen heads craned its neck down towards them, but Carl jumped up and WHAM, biffed the creeper queen head right in the chin.

"SKRRRRRAAAAA!!!!" the head screamed.

Jean-Cowphio was almost high enough to reach the hole, Dave saw. Just five or six more blocks and he'd be high enough. But then, to Dave's horror, one of the creeper queen's heads spotted the cowman.

"SKRRRRIIIIII!!!!!"

All three of the creeper queen's heads turned, twisting their long necks and looking at Jean-Cowphio. Jean-Cowphio stopped building his tower, looking at the heads with terror.

Then FWOOOSHHH!!!! All three creeper queens fired jets of lava at Jean-Cowphio with their mouths. Jean-Cowphio jumped off of the tower he'd built, and the lava jets smashed into the side of the cavern, blasting it wide open.

"Carl!" Dave yelled, pointing at the falling Jean-Cowphio. "Catch him!"

Carl ran over as fast as his golem suit would take him. Dave and Spidroth watched as Carl ran over, then jumped up and grabbed Jean-Cowphio in mid-air, before landing safely on the ground.

The creeper queen had done Jean-Cowphio's job for him, Dave was pleased to see: the lava jets from her three heads had blown a huge hole in the cavern ceiling, and Dave could see the night sky and the stars.

The three huge creeper queen heads all hissed angrily, two of them looking down at Carl and Jean-Cowphio, and one of them looking down at Dave and Spidroth. Dave and Spidroth were surrounded by red creepers again too, all of them slithering towards them.

"Now what?" said Spidroth.

Then Dave heard the sound he'd been waiting to hear: the

sound of hundreds of leathery wings.

"Now we run," he said to Spidroth.

Hundreds upon hundreds of phantoms swooped down through the hole in the cavern roof, attacking everything in sight. The creeper queen roared in anger and pain as the phantoms began biting it. The three heads fired jet after jet of lava out of their mouths, slaughtering phantoms and red creepers alike.

Dave and Spidroth ran over to Carl and Jean-Cowphio.

"Good job, both of you," said Dave. "Now come on, let's get out of here."

The four of them ran towards the passageway that Dave, Jean-Cowphio and Spidroth had first been brought through, leaving the phantoms and the creepers behind to fight it out.

CHAPTER TWELVE

The Top of the Mountain

"You bad boys sure have some crazy adventures," laughed Jean-Cowphio.

The four of them were walking up the side of the mountain. It was still dark, but Dave didn't want to set up camp, especially when there might be more red creepers and phantoms about. He wanted to go up and see the witch, and then get down from the mountain as soon as possible.

"You did well yourself," Dave told Jean-Cowphio. "If it wasn't for you helping to open the hole in the ceiling, we'd probably all be toast by now."

"To be fair, if it wasn't for him we wouldn't even be going up this mountain in the first place," said Carl. "He's the one who angered a crazy witch."

"Guilty as charged," said Jean-Cowphio. "And we're almost there. I gotta say my dudes, your boy Jean-Cowphio is a bit nervous. I dunno how happy Vee is gonna be to see me."

"Remember, the important thing is that you convince her to lift the curse," said Dave.

"You got it, Daddy-o," said Jean-Cowphio. "I'm going to try my best."

Up ahead, Dave could see that they were nearly at the very top of the mountain. In the moonlight he could see a wooden door and windows, which had been built into the side of the stone slope. There were even some flowers in pots outside, and lots and lots of wolves, all hanging around the entrance.

"Vee loves wolves," said Jean-Cowphio.

As they got nearer, the wolves saw them and started running over.

"Weapons ready!" said Dave, pulling out his sword.

"Relax," grinned Jean-Cowphio. "These guys are friendly."

The wolves ran up to Jean-Cowphio and began licking him. Dave noticed that they were all wearing purple collars.

"Good to see you guys!" laughed Jean-Cowphio. "Where's your mummy, hey? Where's your mummy?"

Accompanied by the wolves, Dave, Carl, Spidroth and Jean-Cowphio walked up to the wooden door.

"Ok," said Jean-Cowphio, taking a deep breath. "Here goes."

And he knocked.

At first there was no response, but then Dave could hear someone moving about inside. Then the door swung open to reveal a woman. Her clothes were scruffy brown rags that looked a bit worse for wear and she was holding a half-eaten pumpkin pie in one hand, but those were the least extraordinary things about her. She wasn't a villager, like the other witches Dave had seen, and she wasn't wearing a pointed hat. She had purple skin, short gray hair and eyes of solid white.

"Vee!" said Jean-Cowphio, holding out his arms for a hug. "It's good to see you baby!"

But the purple women pushed past him, walking straight up to Spidroth. There was a look on Spidroth's face that Dave had never seen before: she was *happy*, grinning from ear to ear.

"Spidroth," said the purple woman, an amazed look on her face.

"Vioroth," said Spidroth. Dave was amazed to see that she was crying.

"Ok, this has all got a bit STR-ANGE," said Jean-Cowphio. "What's going on here?"

"Dave, Carl," said Spidroth, "I want you to meet... I want you to meet..."

She was so overcome with tears and emotion that she couldn't even speak.

"This is Viorothbrine," said Spidroth finally. "This is my sister!"

EPILOGUE

Darkest Night wiped the sweat from his brow. It had been a long day.

"Well done, all of you," said Master Seth. "I know we trained hard today, but we need to keep our skills up, even when we don't have any missions."

"But we haven't had a mission in aaaaaages," said Mike. "Where are all the bad guys?"

"Yeah," agreed Alice. "It's been two weeks since we defeated Pumpkin Head and his goons. We've just been doing nothing ever since."

The Ninja Squad was gathered in the jungle underneath their treehouse base. Their old base, which had been destroyed by the Evil Ninjas, had been rebuilt, bigger and better than before. They'd installed redstone lifts into the trees as well, so they could easily get up and down.

"You must all be patient," Seth the Elf said kindly. "A true ninja doesn't go looking for a fight. We are protectors, not soldiers."

"Mooo!" said Master Cowbagio.

"See," laughed Master Seth, stroking the cow on the back of the neck. "Master Cowbagio gets it. Now come on, let's all go home and rest."

"See you losers back in the treehouse," grinned Alice, who was currently in her green lizard form. She flapped her wings and flew into the air.

"Not if I get there first," grinned Darkest Night, transforming his body into black smoke and flying after her.

That evening it was Ash's turn to cook, so he made them all cooked porkchops, with a little help in the kitchen from his electric cat. Like Master Seth, Ash made sure his Elemental Block power was activated at all times, as his cat had been created by the block, so if his power ran out it would disappear. Elemental Block powers ran out after one day if they weren't replenished, so Ash always made sure he charged up his powers every morning.

Master Seth had an even more vital reason for using the Elemental Block every day. He had been created by the block, pulled from the mind of a creeper named Carl, and charging his powers with the Elemental Block every day was the only thing that stopped him from fading out of existence.

After dinner, Darkest Night went to his dorm room and started reading the latest *Seth the Elf* comic in bed. Jackson had gone to New Diamond City recently to get them all copies of the new issue, but Darkest Night wasn't very impressed with it. There was a new character in the comic, a wizard called AlexCakeLover6000, who was ridiculously overpowered. Not only could she fly and breathe fire-lighting from her mouth, but she could somehow hold a million swords in one hand.

Darkest Night was about half way through the comic when he started to nod off, and soon he was asleep. He was in the middle of a lovely dream about pumpkin pie when he was woken by shouting coming from somewhere outside.

Darkest Night ran out of his dorm room and saw that huge portions of the treehouse were on fire. The other ninjas had all run out of their rooms too, and were looking up at the sky.

A huge shape was circling above them in the dark night sky.

"It's a dragon!" shouted Chase.

"Everyone power up!" shouted Master Seth.

Darkest Night tried to turn himself into smoke, and realized that yes, his powers had run out while he was sleeping.

He and all the other ninjas ran towards the small temple made of gold blocks, where the Elemental Block was kept. They were almost there when suddenly a blast of fire from above sent them flying backwards.

Darkest Night landed painfully on the wooden floor of the treehouse. The other ninjas were lying all around him, and nearly all the treehouse was on fire now.

The only ninjas left standing were Ash and Master Seth, who both still had their powers.

"Go Electropaws!" Ash yelled. "I believe in you!"

"Meow!" Ash's yellow cat shouted, then *FWAASH!* It blasted the dragon with a bolt of lightning. For a moment the sky lit up, and Darkest Night saw that the dragon was made of diamond.

It's the Ancient's dragon! he realized. And a jolt of fear went down him.

Comics hadn't been the only thing that Jackson had brought back from New Diamond City: he'd also brought back news. While there he'd heard that the city had been attacked by a diamond dragon ridden by an old man. The people of New Diamond City had no clue where the dragon had come from or who the old man was, but they did know one thing: Herobrine had slain the old man, stolen the dragon and flown off.

Darkest night knew that the old man must have been the Ancient, which meant there could only be one person flying that dragon:

Herobrine.

Suddenly the treehouse began to collapse, and Darkest Night found himself falling through the air, surrounded by burning wood and ninjas, towards the jungle floor below.

WHAM!

Darkest Night hit the ground hard. He looked around and saw all his fellow ninjas on the ground around him. Like him, they were injured, but had thankfully survived the fall. All of them were awake, apart from Oof, who was lying unconscious next to him. Darkest Night crawled over to Oof to check he was ok, and was pleased to find he was still breathing.

Then something else hit the ground in the middle of the ninjas: a glowing, colorful block.

"It's the Elemental Block!" yelled Guyjack.

Mike was nearest, so he crawled over to the block, placing his hands on it.

Suddenly there was a blinding flash of white light. Then, when Darkest Night could see again, he saw Mike was on his feet, holding the block and grinning.

"I've got my super speed back!" said Mike.

"Hath thee lost control of thine senses, fool?" roared Kyle the

Mighty. "Hurry up and let us use the block too!"

"Oh yeah," said Mike.

Then *ZIP, ZIP, ZIP*, he zipped around, letting all the other members of the ninjas touch the block. There was flash after flash of white light, then all the Ninja Squad were on their feet, ready for battle and fully powered. Even Master Cowbagio the cow was ready, his eyes glowing green with his grass powers.

"The dragon is coming!" Master Seth yelled.

He was right, Darkest Night saw. The huge diamond dragon was swooping down towards them. The jungle around them was all on fire now, and the night sky was lit with orange light.

FSSHAM! Master Cowbagio fired his green eye beams at the dragon, but they reflected off its diamond body. Electropaws the cat fired a bolt of electricity at it, but it barely made the dragon flinch.

The dragon was almost on them now, and they could see orange fire glowing down its throat, getting ready to blast them.

"Guyjack!" yelled Master Seth. "Ice shield!"

Guyjack ran forward in his blue robes and *FWOOOSH*, he sprayed ice from his fingers, creating an ice wall. The dragon breathed fire at them, but the ice wall blocked it, and steam filled the air.

Then *KRASH!* The dragon smashed through the ice wall with its head. It had landed now and was walking on all fours, and Darkest Night saw Herobrine riding on its neck. As he looked into Herobrine's cold white eyes, he felt a chill run down his spine.

"Destroy the dragon! Slay the rider!" Master Seth roared. "Use everything you've got!"

The Ninja Squad charged into action.

Alice, now in her green flying lizard form, swooped down

towards Herobrine, but the diamond dragon swung its diamond head up and grabbed her in its jaws, before swinging its neck and throwing her into a tree trunk: *SLAM!*

DJ, Guyjack and Jolt Flame all began blasting the dragon with their sound, ice and fire powers, while Lila and Sasha fired arrows at it with their powerful bows, Kyle fired lightning at it with his sword and Ash's cat blasted it with electricity.

Darkest Night was going to get involved himself, but then he realized his nightmare powers would be better saved for Herobrine, not the mindless robotic dragon.

Then, while the dragon was flailing around and distracted by all the attacks, Avyukth-San jumped down from a nearby tree, with both of his huge glowing red axes. Then *FWLANG!* He used both his axes to chop the diamond dragon's head clean off.

Immediately the dragon exploded, diamond blocks going everywhere.

"We did it, dudes!" yelled DJ.

"The battle's not over yet," said Master Seth. "Look."

Herobrine was walking towards them through the ruins of the treehouse and the shattered blocks of dragon. Behind him, the jungle burned.

"You must be the Ninja Squad," he said softly. "Well met."

Herobrine's voice was soft, but there was something about it that made Darkest Night's head hurt. He suddenly found himself recalling all his most painful memories and thinking about how futile and pointless life was. It was like Herobrine's voice was sucking out all the happiness and love in the world, leaving only darkness.

"I'm here for that block of yours," Herobrine continued. "I went to the hidden village of Ninjanos, where I was told the block would be, but when I got there I found it in ruins: just a few stray zombie pigmen and a handful of ninjas. The ninjas told me they had once been part of the Ninjanos Clan, but most of their clan had been defeated and captured, and they were all that was left. And they told me that your clan had stolen the Glitchicon."

"The Glitchy-what?" said Shadow.

"The block you have," said Herobrine. "I want it. If you give it to me, I will let you live. You have my word."

He looked over at the block, which Mike was still holding in his hands.

"If we give it to you, Master Seth will die," said Chase. "We will defend it with our lives."

"Yeah," said Knight Swagger, smashing his fists together, "if you want it, come and get it."

"Ok," said Herobrine. "I will."

And he began to walk forward towards Mike.

"Rrrraaa!!!" Knight Swagger yelled, rushing towards Herobrine.

POW, POW, POW!!! Knight Swagger biffed Herobrine in the face with three mighty punches, but Herobrine didn't even flinch. Knight Swagger's eyes went wide with fear, then Herobrine swatted him with the back of his hand. He'd barely touched Knight Swagger, but the big villager went flying, then *THAM!* He smashed into a tree.

Guyjack, Jolt Flame, DJ, Kyle and Electropaws the cat all blasted Herobrine at once, but their powers didn't seem to be doing anything to him either. Then Herobrine held out his hands and their powers were reflected back at them, sending them all flying.

Maybe some nightmares will knock him out, thought Darkest Night. He turned himself into his usual black cloud, then rushed towards Herobrine, smothering him in darkness.

But instead, Darkest Night found the darkness overcoming *him.* Herobrine's mind was like nothing he'd ever come across before. There were no nightmares or fear there, just pure evil. It was too much for Darkest Night, and he turned back to normal and went rolling across the ground.

"You would do wise to stay out of my head," Herobrine said to him, then he turned and kept walking.

Darkest Night noticed a shadow creeping underneath Herobrine's feet, and then Shadow, Chase, Knight Galaxy and Segid the Skeleton jumped out of it, all attacking Herobrine with their swords. They all hit Herobrine with blow after blow, but it was like they were hitting solid bedrock: Herobrine didn't even flinch. Knight Galaxy even tried barging into Herobrine with his bedrock armor, but it made no difference.

"Let me try!" roared Jackson, and he charged at Herobrine with his horns. But Herobrine just grabbed the horns and swung Jackson into the swordsmen, who all went flying. Then he let go of the horns and Jackson went flying into a tree.

Lila and Sasha fired arrows at Herobrine, but they just bounced off. Herobrine reached out with his hands and both their bows shattered, unleashing small electrical explosions that sent both women flying.

Now the only ninjas left on their feet were Mike, who was holding the Elemental Block, and Master Seth, who was standing guard in front of Mike with his two magic wooden swords. Master Cowbagio the cow was standing with them too.

"Run, Mike," said Master Seth. "Get as far away from here as you can. This villain must never get his hands on the Elemental Block."

"Are you sure?" said Mike. "I can't leave you guys!"

"Go!" roared Seth.

"Ok," said Mike sadly, looking around at the other ninjas. Then he turned and ran... or at least he tried to run. His legs were suddenly tied up with jungle vines coming from the ground. The vines were creeping up Mike's legs, wrapping themselves around his body.

"There is no escaping me," said Herobrine softly.

"Moo!" yelled Master Cowbagio, and the cow fired his green eyes at Herobrine.

Herobrine held a hand up, blocking the green beam, then redirected it back at the cow. Thankfully the beam didn't turn Master Cowbagio into grass, but it knocked her out.

Master Seth charged forward.

"Yaaaaa!" he yelled, jumping through the air and slashing his swords at Herobrine.

CLASSSH!!! Both swords shattered as soon as they hit Herobrine, then Master Seth landed on the ground. Herobrine raised his hands and vines wrapped themselves around Seth as well, pinning him down.

Mike was completely smothered by vines now, so Herobrine just reached forward and took the Elemental Block off of him.

Then Herobrine dug his fingers into the Elemental Block... and tore it in two.

FWWOOOOOOOOOOOOOOSSSH!!!!!!!!!

There was a gigantic blast of white light. Darkest Night felt his powers start to get weaker. He still had them, but he could feel them quickly fading away.

"You see?" Herobrine said to the fallen ninjas. "That wasn't too hard."

"What's going on?" said a confused voice. Darkest Night turned around and saw that Oof had woken up.

"It's Herobrine," Darkest Night whispered to Oof. "He's destroyed the Elemental Block. We tried to defeat him, but he's too strong."

"I know how to defeat him!" Oof whispered excitedly. "Master Carl told me how they defeated him back in Diamond City! Hopefully the potion chest survived the fall."

Then *BWAMF!* Oof teleported away in a blast of purple smoke.

"The power," Herobrine said, looking at his hands, "I feel even more powerful than before!"

He rose up into the sky, hovering in mid-air.

"And I can fly now!" he grinned. "I used to be able to float a bit, but this is so much better."

BWAMF! Oof appeared on the ground below Herobrine, holding an armful of splash potions.

"I'm afraid your flying days are over," Oof shouted at Herobrine. Then he threw a splash potion, hitting Herobrine right in the face.

BWAMF! BWAMF! BWAMF! BWAMF! BWAMF! Oof teleported around Herobrine, throwing splash potions at him from every angle. Soon Herobrine was dripping with blue-gray liquid.

"Feeling a bit slow, are you?" Oof grinned, standing on the ground and looking up at Herobrine. "Do you feel like sleeping?"

"No, actually," said Herobrine. "But thank you. Now I know for sure that I'm immune to potions."

Oof's face went white with fear.

Herobrine held his hand out and Oof's remaining splash potion bottles shattered into pieces. Oof was coated in slowness potion, and he collapsed.

"Goodbye, ninjas," said Herobrine. "I'd kill you, but why bother? Without your powers you're nothing."

And then Herobrine rose off into the sky, flying away and disappearing from sight.

Darkest Night staggered to his feet. He felt the last of his powers draining from him. Soon they would be gone for good.

"Is everyone ok?" he shouted.

It looked like everyone was. The other ninjas were all pulling themselves to their feet as well. They were all injured and worse for wear, but alive.

But then Darkest Night heard something that chilled him to his core.

"Master Seth!" Mike was yelling. "What's happening to you?!"

All the Ninja Squad ran over. Seth the Elf, their master, was kneeling on the floor, and he was fading away. His body was so faint that Darkest Night could see through him.

"Without the Elemental Block... I cannot exist..." said Master Seth, his voice sounding weak and far away. "Before I go... you have all been excellent students... and you are fine ninjas..."

And then Master Seth was gone.

"No!" said Segid, falling to his knees.

Some of the ninjas started crying, others just hugged each other. Darkest Night just felt hollow, like there was an empty hole inside of him.

"What do we do now?" Chase said sadly. "How can we go on without a master? Without our powers?"

Darkest Night had no idea. But then, to his surprise, he heard a voice he didn't recognize.

"Hey, are you guys ok?" said the voice. "And this is going to sound like a weird question... but do you have any cake?"

TO BE CONTINUED...

Made in the USA
Coppell, TX
03 February 2024

28547638R00052